we *playfully dedicate this book to our*
families of origin and creation:

al

brian

stephen

jena

pat

evelyn

jim

ralph

dan

sandy

chanry

rache

jim

kurt

ellen

glenn

jared

ross

bill

dave

jennifer

allison

shannon

renée

lorene

bob

kent

chris

roberta

eddie

jessica

mary jo

ron

sluggo

tom

brynn

helen

catharine

delynn

miksiw

aura

tagen

keith

mr. lion

brewster

harrison

keith

ginny

Harrison, Marvel • Kellogg, Terry • Michaels, Greg

ISBN 1-880257-01-7

Printed in the United States of America

Other books offered by BRAT Publishing:

Finding Balance *12 Priorities For Interdependence and Joyful Living:*
Terry Kellogg & Marvel Harrison

Broken Toys Broken Dreams *Understanding and Healing Boundaries, Codependence,
Compulsion & Family Relationships:* Terry Kellogg

AttrACTIVE WOMEN *A Physical Fitness Approach To Emotional & Spiritual Well-Being:*
Marvel Harrison & Catharine Stewart-Roache

Butterfly Kisses *Little Intimacies For Sharing!* Harrison & Kellogg & Michaels

Hummingbird Words *Self Affirmations & Notes To Nurture By:* Harrison & Kellogg & Michaels

Roots & Wings *Words For Growing A Family:* Harrison & Kellogg & Michaels

BRAT Publishing, Suite 225, 6 University Drive, Amherst, MA 01002
1-800-359-BRAT (2728)

roots and wings

notes on growing a family

marvel harrison   terry kellogg

illustrations by greg michaels

BRAT PUBLISHING

*h*ave you ever found people with whom you felt safe enough to be yourself? people who accepted you for who you are, believed in you while nurturing your journey? a family brought us to life, a family brings us to life.

*i*n family we learn to live and play, love and pray. family are the people we can always come home to.

*o*ur roots are planted in family - of origin or creation. when we are firmly grounded we can spread our wings and soar.

listen with your eyes

listen to their eyes

laugh at the sound of laughter

*e*mbrace differences

acknowledge strengths

affirm uniqueness

*r*ead aloud read alone

breed music

give time take time

balance attention

baby's job is to express needs

parent's job is to listen to babies

kids hear and respond even when we don't think so

*M*ake believe

play dress up

do picnics and parades

puppy wrestle

*b*e consistent not predictable

be active not reactive

allow consequences

affirm feelings when you can't affirm behavior

*d*on't be mean

don't be obscene

don't lean

don't litter

*S*elf disclose

let your family know who you are

let your family know where you are

model emotional fluency

*S*prinkle hope

sparkle courage

spackle confidence

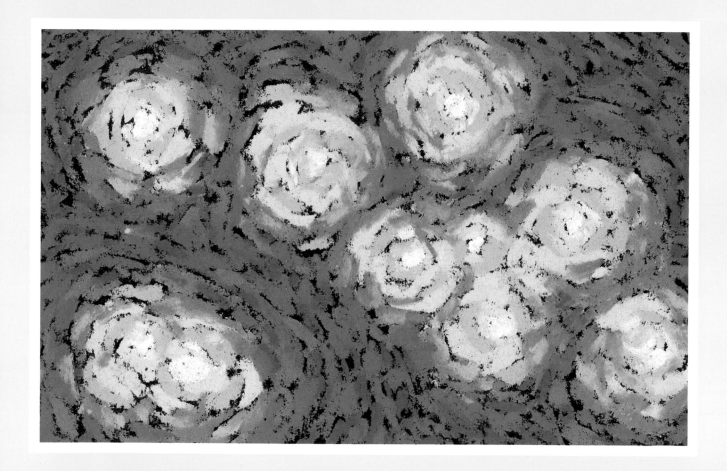

*V*alidate and investigate conflict

take it seriously don't panic

teach process time

when all else fails. . .breathe!

*t*ease gently

say each other's names

use terms of endearment

*C*hildren will do it when they are ready
responsibilities are earned not assigned
encourage and acknowledge work
play is the work of children we are all children

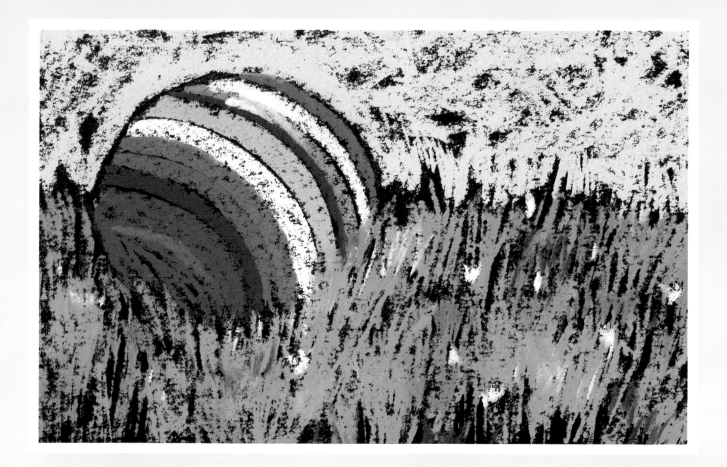

*C*herish life

adopt a pet

feed and neuter your pet

demand respect for creation

*k*eep rules to a minimum

expect basic courtesies

reach toward not away

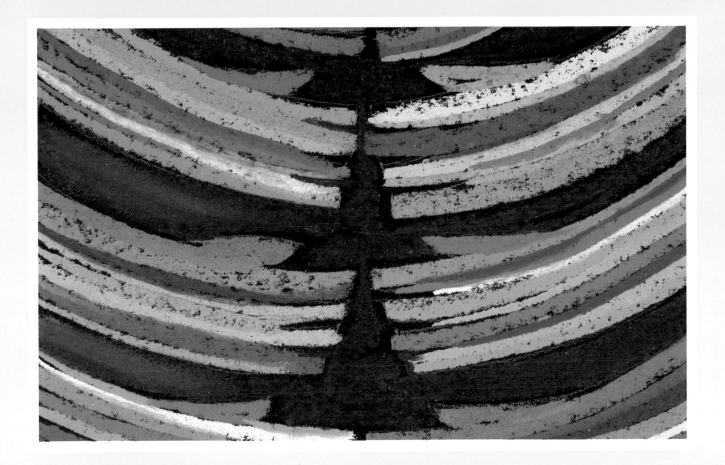

*n*otice

touch

mirror

guide

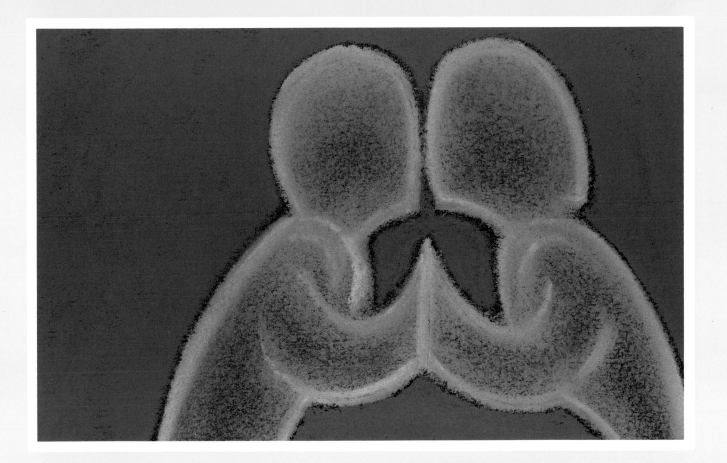

*t*alking is like checkers take turns

discuss openly sex luv and other four letter words

leave notes

let the fridge be a family billboard

*a*sk questions

get directions

request permission

say what you need

*l*et people resolve differences

apologize and seek forgiveness

share your losses

use outside resources

*n*o hitting

no fibbing

no finger pointing

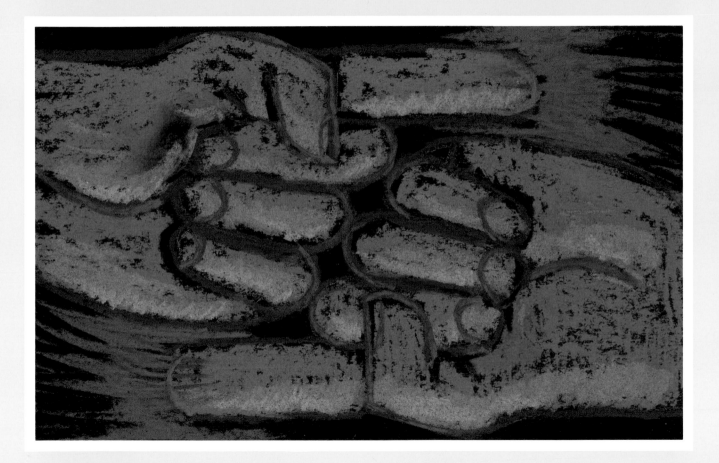

find family fitness

hang around active families

play outside

jump for joy!

*S*hare gratitude don't seek it

appeal to values

nurture spirit and spirituality

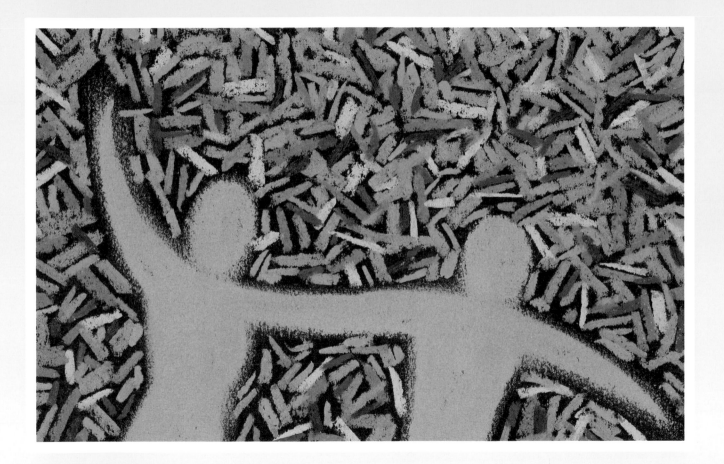

*S*hare stories

chronicle and treasure memories

value tradition

*g*o together

let the world in

nourish humor

enhance hope

deliver dreams

*d*ear creator

may we embrace that we are all one family

may we protect and cherish our home the earth

Marvel Harrison, a native of Canada, is an avid runner, skier, canoeist and likes to play. She is a PhD candidate in Counseling Psychology, author, therapist and lecturer specializing in a gentle approach to self acceptance. She is an eating disorder consultant and a program trainer for Baywood Hospital in Webster, Texas. Marvel's spirit and zest for life are easily felt by audiences everywhere.

Terry Kellogg is a parent, athlete, counselor and teacher. For twenty years he has been helping families with compulsive and addictive behaviors. Besides writing poetry, he is a wilderness enthusiast, an advocate for vulnerable groups and our planet. He is a national education consultant and a trainer for Baywood Hospital in Webster, Texas. Terry is an entertaining, challenging, inspiring and much sought after speaker.

Gregory Michaels is a full time Dad and a free lance illustrator. His clever wit and sensitivity to children of all ages are apparent in his work and he has a terrific sense of humor to boot! Greg and his family make their home in the Rocky Mountains of Colorado.